Your Happiest YOU

The Care & Keeping of Your Mind and Spirit

by Judy Woodburn
illustrated by Josée Masse

*Jane Annunziata, PsyD, and Lori Gustafson, MS
consultants*

★ American Girl®

With thanks to Madison Insight Meditation Group,
whose kind and quiet company helped
this book take shape. —J.W.

Published by American Girl Publishing
No part of this book may be used or reproduced in any
manner whatsoever without written permission except in the case
of brief quotations embodied in critical articles and reviews.

17 18 19 20 21 22 23 24 QP 10 9 8 7 6 5 4 3 2 1

Editorial Development: Darcie Johnston
Art Direction and Design: Sarah Jane Boecher
Illustrations: Josée Masse
Production: Jeannette Bailey, Caryl Boyer, Lisa Bunescu,
Jessica Rogers, Cynthia Stiles

Library of Congress Cataloging-in-Publication Data
LC record available at https://lccn.loc.gov/2016042039

americangirl.com/service

Dear Reader,

By now, you're getting pretty good at taking care of yourself. You eat your veggies and brush your teeth. You try to get exercise and rest. Even now, you're building habits you'll use all your life to care for your body, keep it strong, and be your healthiest you.

Did you know that your mind can use a little care and keeping, too? Of course, your brain benefits from all the ways you keep your body healthy. But having a few good mental habits can also help a girl have a happier life—a life with lots of meaning and joy.

This book is full of information that will help you understand your developing mind and brain. It's also full of simple tips and fun activities to help you nurture your mind just the way you've begun to care for your physical self. We hope that learning these habits makes it easier for you to feel connected to the people in your life, stay focused on what really matters, and bounce back quickly when things don't go right. We hope it helps you feel calm and content inside—no matter how crazy things get on the outside.

Your friends at American Girl

Table of Contents

GROWING UP HAPPY
page 6

HAPPINESS HABIT 1
LETTING IT SETTLE
page 14

HAPPINESS HABIT 2
TUNING IN
page 30

HAPPINESS HABIT 3
CARING AND CONNECTING
page 50

HAPPINESS HABIT 4
FINDING YOUR WAY
page 66

HAPPINESS HABIT 5
LOOKING FOR WHAT'S GOOD
page 84

HAPPINESS HABIT 6
KEEPING A GOOD THING GOING
page 106

GROWING UP HAPPY

I am going through puberty, and it isn't going well. Please give me some good advice I can use and be HAPPY.
—Lauren

Who's Happy?

You are, of course, whenever good things happen. In moments like these, you know just what happy is: It's exclamation points!!! It's sunny and fizzy and fabulous. It's the kind of feeling you wish could last forever.

Me, with MY prize-winning chocolate-berry-almond pancakes!

Our book bowl team got (nearly) every answer right!

BFF
M.J.
L.N.

Mykel isn't moving six states away after all!

Now that you're getting older, though, you also know that every day brings something different. Sure, there are days you want in your scrapbook—amazing days when everything goes right. There are easy days when you feel relaxed and comfy in your own skin. But there are also lots of days you'd love to crumple up and forget. As you're growing up, you may be discovering that feeling great just isn't possible all the time.

Here's the good news . . .

Getting older means you can start to think about **happy** in a new and deeper way.

9

Learning New Steps

For a while now, experts have been studying what makes people happy, deep down. One thing they know for sure is that being happy isn't only about having a lot of good things happen to you. Happy has a lot to do with how you respond to what happens, no matter what comes your way.

Happy is bouncing back when you've gotten knocked down. It's knowing that problems *will* happen and feeling confident you'll be able to deal with them.

Happy is feeling connected to the people in your life—to friends and family, and even to people you might not know very well.

Happy is accepting that it's normal *not* to feel happy all the time, and knowing it'll pass.

In fact, happy's not just something you feel. It's also something you *do*. It's a bit like a dance. And just like dancing, happiness has steps you can learn.

11

Your Helpful Habits

WAKE

How do you get ready for bed at night? Do you put on your pajamas first or brush your teeth? Do you read for a bit or turn out the light right away? Chances are, you don't pay much attention to these things. You just do them. They are habits.

SHORTCUT

Teeth

BUS

If you've ever struggled to stop nibbling your nails or cracking your knuckles, you might tend to think of habits as "bad." Not always! Habits are all the things you do each day without really thinking about them. Habits are your brain's way of taking shortcuts. Without them, you'd have to think through every little thing you did. Your brain would be worn out by breakfast!

LESSON

LOCKER

Because your brain relies on habits to guide you through your day, habits influence everything from how you eat to how you speak and move. Habits even affect what you think and how you respond to what happens to you. So, for something you don't think about much, habits can have a surprisingly big say in how you feel. That's why it's important to begin building the kind of habits that will help you feel good.

Ready to learn how?
Read on!

Sometimes I get these really crazy
mood swings, and I feel like I hate
everyone or need to cry for no reason.
It's not helping that I have a bunch
of tests and projects right now. Ugh!
—Alesya

HAPPINESS
HABIT 1

LETTING IT SETTLE

All Shook Up

Your mind and a snow globe: They don't seem to have much in common. But lots of people say they do. If you watch a snow globe for a minute or two, it's easy to see why.

What happens when you give a snow globe a good shake? Flakes fly every-where, of course. When the snow's really stirred up, it can be hard even to see who or what's at the center. Our minds can get like that, too—thoughts and feelings swirling this way and that. Sometimes they're so stirred up that we can't see our own situation very clearly, either.

You know how it feels when your mind's stirred up. When you get invited to two parties on the same day. When Aris gets the drum solo after you prac-ticed harder. When parents are arguing. When Elise, who you thought was a friend, forms a homework club that doesn't include you. It's awfully hard to make decisions or handle problems when there's a storm swirling inside you.

If you could somehow keep from ever getting jostled or stressed, you might be able to keep any mental blizzards from happening. The truth is, that's just not possible. Some days stir up irritation, impatience, or uncertainty. Other days bring more intense feelings like sadness, anxiety, or anger. One thing's guaran-teed, though: Every girl gets shaken up by something.

Storm Warnings

Do everyday troubles shake you up a little or a lot?
Give each situation your personal storm rating.

1. Your dolphin jigsaw puzzle has 1,001 pieces in 1,000 shades of gray. It took you three weeks to put it together . . . and it's taken your little sister three seconds to fling it apart.

a. major blizzard
b. a few flurries
c. clear skies

2. Mr. Yao, Mr. Bitterburst, and Ms. Leinhosen must be conspiring. How else could you have a science test, a book report, and a history project due on the same day—again?

a. major blizzard
b. a few flurries
c. clear skies

3. Aisha's mom thinks bronzer and colored lip balm don't count as makeup. Your mom says they do, and there's no way you're wearing them to school.

a. major blizzard
b. a few flurries
c. clear skies

4. Yesterday you got up the courage to tell Camrelle that you kind of like A.J. Today A.J. told Camrelle that he kind of likes Mimi.

a. major blizzard
b. a few flurries
c. clear skies

5. Your parents can't agree on where you're spending Thanksgiving—Mom's house or Dad's. You're starting to feel like a wishbone about to be tugged in two.

a. major blizzard
b. a few flurries
c. clear skies

6. No. That strip of toilet paper has not been hanging from the waistband of your jeans for the entire last hour.

a. major blizzard
b. a few flurries
c. clear skies

Answers

Did you have lots of **a's** or **b's?** You're hardly alone. What rattles you may be completely different from what rattles a friend, but every girl runs into rough weather and needs a few ways to help the storms inside her settle. How can you do that? It all begins with your breath.

Catching Your Breath

What's your breathing like, right this second? If you're curled up in a chair and feeling relaxed, your breaths are probably slow and gentle. Next time you're mad—really mad!—or watching a scary part in a movie, or riding a roller coaster as it's chugging up the tallest hill of the track, you might notice that something's different. Your breathing may be faster. Or maybe, without even having decided to . . .

you . . . are . . . holding

your . . . breath.

This happens because the way we breathe helps our bodies and brains respond to whatever's going on around or inside us. When you're excited, mad, or scared, you tend to suck in air and breathe faster, which charges up your nervous system. This revving up can be super-useful—if you need to run a race or dash away from a situation.

Of course, the things that most often stir up a girl's day—drama with friends, an unfinished book report, or a disagreement with parents—aren't things she can physically run from. She can't just get rid of the uncomfortable feelings that come up in these situations, either.

So what's a girl to do? It really helps if you can find a way to stop fighting the swirling thoughts and feelings and simply let them settle, like flakes in a snow globe. When you're able to do that, you can see your way clear to deal with the problem.

Luckily, your breath can help here, too.

Breathing Easy

Start by noticing what happens when you breathe. You don't need to make your breaths deeper or longer, or change them at all. Just see how your breathing feels. Are your breaths slow or fast? Do you feel your chest or belly expand when you breathe in? Does the air feel cool as it passes through your nose or mouth?

These are things we don't usually notice. But here's an amazing fact: Simply tuning in to your breathing can help you start to feel less jangled.

You can settle yourself even more by doing this simple breathing exercise:

Take a slow, deep breath in through your nose.

Let your belly swell as you breathe in.

Then, as you let the air out through your mouth, picture yourself gently blowing on a dandelion.

Imagine the seeds floating lazily on a soft breeze.

Try this a few more times. You may start to notice that your breath wants to take a little pause just after you've exhaled. If so, let yourself enjoy this tiny moment of quiet and calm before you breathe in again.

By paying attention to your breath, and by breathing deeply and slowly, you are helping to trigger a different part of your nervous system—the part that loosens you up and calms you down.

How do things feel now?

Moving Past a Storm

Powerful emotions like anger and worry do more than rev up your breathing. They make your muscles clench up, too. And when muscles stay tense, they can even start to hurt—which means a headache, stomach ache, or backache might not be far behind. (As if you weren't stressed enough already!)

The exercises here let your body calm itself by helping those tense muscles unclench. Tuning in to how your body feels when you do these movements doesn't just help your body feel better. It can also settle your mind and even boost a gloomy mood.

Find Your Balance

This is a great way to practice feeling steady, inside and out. Start by standing on two feet. Then carefully lift one foot up to rest on the inside of the other leg. You can rest your foot low on your calf, or higher up, above your knee. Do what's comfortable, and feel free to use your arms to steady yourself. When you're ready, try raising your arms over your head. Don't worry if you tip. Finding your balance again is part of the exercise!

Shake It Off

When a latch is stuck tight, sometimes the only way to loosen it is to jiggle it. And sometimes, when strong feelings are making your muscles tense, a little jiggling will loosen them up, too. Try it! Stand with your knees slightly bent, and start bouncing lightly. Let your arms and hands bounce along. Bounce slowly at first, then faster and faster. Feel the jiggle in your arms, legs, belly, and even your cheeks and lips. When you're ready to stop, let the jiggling get slower and slower—as if you're a wind-up toy that's winding down.

The One-Girl Hug

A warm hug can feel comforting when you're stressed—even if it comes from yourself! Wrap your arms around your body and give yourself a friendly squeeze. If you like, add on a soothing mini-massage: Briskly rub your hands together until they're warm, and then gently massage your forehead, temples, and neck. *Mmmmm.*

Stretch for the Sun

If you're feeling down, moving your body can lift you back up! In this exercise, imagine yourself as a tree in springtime, growing toward the warm sun.

Start by standing with your feet a bit apart.

Bend forward, starting with your head . . .

then your shoulders . . .

then your waist.

Let your head and arms dangle loosely for a few seconds.

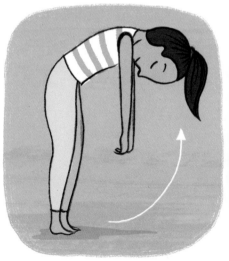

Now, slowly straighten back up, letting your arms hang down.

Once you're standing straight, begin lifting your arms slowly out to your sides, as if they're branches of a tree.

Reach your arms high overhead and look up, as if the sun is shining on your face. Feel yourself growing inside.

Just Rest

In yoga, there's a relaxing position that's called "the child" because little kids often sleep this way. To try it, kneel on a rug or mat and bend forward, letting your forehead or cheek rest on the floor. Let your arms relax down along your sides. Breathe deeply and feel the floor underneath your body, stable and firm.

After any exercise, check in with your body and breathing. How are they feeling right this moment?

Peaceful Inside

How do you relax when you're feeling stressed out or wound up? What helps you settle yourself?

I try to calm down by reading a book and organizing my room.
—Molly

My favorite place to go when I need time to think is a nice hot bath! It is soothing and relaxing, and I can think about things without a lot of noise.
—Naomi

I take a deep breath and think.
—Alejandra

I go to my piano. Music always helps clear my mind.
—Jolie

I sit on my bed and pull out my journal.
—Savannah

I listen to my favorite music. This always makes me happy.
—Karen

I like to go outside and cuddle a pet. The fresh air feels good, and animals make me feel calm.
—Elle

I like taking walks in our woods because they are so beautiful and peaceful. It's a place where I can really sort out my problems.
—Sophia

I go outside in my backyard and climb my favorite tree. I sit on the sturdiest branch and think there. I stare out in the big open grass. I notice how quiet and beautiful nature is.
—Mia

When I need a break from stress, I surround myself with nature. I sit under my favorite tree, which I named, and I write, read, or doodle the hours away.
—Janani

I like to tell my doll how I'm feeling. It makes me feel so much better. I feel more confident, too.
—Chloe

HAPPINESS
HABIT 2
TUNING IN

MY phone is really distracting! I love reading on it, or looking at social media. I procrastinate a LOT!
—Alexandra

Find Fiona

Fiona

Meet Fiona. She's a girl a lot like you. Fiona needs to focus on her science textbook for a big test on Friday. The test counts for one-quarter of her grade! But life isn't making it easy for her to study. Can you find Fiona amid everything that's distracting her?

RISTORANTE

Candy

PET

Found!

Did you spot Fiona in the window of the À La Moda building? If so, how?

Your brain has two ways of paying attention. One is for protecting you. It makes you "snap to" when a door slams, a glass breaks, or anything else happens that makes you feel surprised or unsure. Bright colors and movement grab your attention this way, too. Long ago, when humans scrounged for food in the wild, it was important to notice things like bright berries or swimming fish that were good to eat.

Nowadays, the fast-moving, colorful things are often on screens—like movies and video games. And many of the things a girl can feel unsure about are also on screens—in social websites and apps. Things like this are sticky like glue: They grab your attention and hold it.

Your brain's second way of paying attention is one that lets you *choose* what to focus on. This kind of attention is like a spotlight you aim on things that are important to you. It's the kind that Fiona's trying to use to read her book, and it's the kind you used to find her. This kind of attention requires an extra-heaping dose of brain energy. That's why focusing on things that aren't "sticky" can be really hard sometimes.

It may be hard—but it's also one of the best mental habits a girl can have.

Your Personal Superpower

What makes attention so important for feeling happy?

Being able to hold something steady with your attention is like a real-life superpower. Why? Because aiming your attention makes it possible for you to do what you set out to do.

A bajillion things happen around us all the time—too much for any brain to take in. Your attention power lets you decide what matters to you, while the rest fades into the background. In fact, since no one else chooses exactly the same things to focus on, attention is one of the main things that make you *you*.

Experts who study happiness know that when you're distracted, it's harder to make choices that you'll feel good about later. By using your powers of attention, you can aim your energy at things that will help you grow up happy—and away from things that won't.

Tuned In or Zoned Out?

Can you see yourself in any of these girls?

1. You're thrilled to bump into a friend at your cousin's party. Still, you can't help gazing over her shoulder while she's talking. *Who else is here?* you wonder. *What's that song that's playing? Are any of those cheese thingies left on the snack table?*
   a. That's not me.
   b. It's a bit like me.
   c. It's a lot like me.

2. While your Spanish teacher was explaining the six steps for making sugar skulls, you were thinking about the test in science next hour. "Any questions?" asks Señor Swivet. *Yes!* you think. *What were steps 1, 2, 3, 4, and, um, 5?*
   a. That's not me.
   b. It's a bit like me.
   c. It's a lot like me.

3. *Thunk!* That was your elbow, crashing into the door frame because you weren't looking where you were going.
   a. That's not me.
   b. It's a bit like me.
   c. It's a lot like me.

4. *The Mistriver Chronicle* has everything you love in a book—a fuzzy alien, a nymph who reads minds, and a girl who builds robots—but you're having trouble getting into it. You keep catching yourself rereading the same paragraphs or skimming over some pages completely.
a. That's not me.
b. It's a bit like me.
c. It's a lot like me.

5. Most days, the word that would best describe your bedroom is "half": the bed is half-made, half of your clean clothes are still in the laundry basket, and a half-finished beading project has been on your desk since your birthday before last.
a. That's not me.
b. It's a bit like me.
c. It's a lot like me.

6. You're nibbling from a dish of salty peanuts while you browse on the Internet. You reach for another and . . . hey! The dish is empty! Did you finish the whole thing already?
a. That's not me.
b. It's a bit like me.
c. It's a lot like me.

Answers

Did you choose many **b's** or **c's?** Chances are, you had at least a few. Your mind may not always be where *you* are, especially when you need to focus on things that aren't super-interesting. This is hard for everyone, young and old, but it's especially tough for kids because their brains are still developing. Luckily, attention is like any skill—playing an instrument, turning a cartwheel, baking a cake. Even kids who struggle to focus can get better with practice.

Training Your Brain

How do you teach a playful puppy to sit? Each time the puppy pops up or starts to scamper off, you gently pull it back and start again. And each time the puppy does what you want him to—even for a second—you make sure to reward him. Good puppy! Well done!

Experts say that your attention is a bit like that puppy. It wants to chase squirrels, fetch tennis balls, or sniff whatever is most interesting at the moment. But with a little training, your brain can get better at aiming your attention where you want it to go.

One way to train your brain is to practice paying attention—really tuning in—to something. Your breath is a great thing to practice with. Noticing how your breath feels can help you feel calmer—which can make it easier to pay attention. And there's nothing more handy than your breath: Wherever you go, it comes along!

Here's how to get started.

1. Get comfortable. Sit on the floor, on a pillow, or on a chair—whatever feels best to you. Or you can lie on your back if that feels better.

2. Take a few deep breaths through your nose, and see if you can zero in on how your breath feels. You might feel it best in the tip of your nose. Or you might feel it best in your belly as it moves in and out. You can rest your hands gently on your belly, if that helps you tune in better. Closing your eyes may help you tune in better, too, but it's not necessary.

3. Now take five breaths. That's it. Just five. See if you can keep your attention focused on the feeling of the breath in your nose or your belly as you breathe in and out.

If you notice that you're thinking about something else, bring your focus back to your breathing, the way you'd call back a playful puppy. And just the way you'd praise the puppy for doing what you want, give yourself a little mental pat on the back.

As you breathe out each breath, count it silently in your head . . .

1...2...3...4...5...

Five breaths. What could be simpler? Give it a try right now!

Distraction in Action

Did you try the attention exercise? If so, you probably noticed that staying focused on your breathing isn't all that easy. Distractions are everywhere!

They can pop up **around you.** Suddenly you might feel like you need to look at things you've hardly glanced at before. Sounds might bother you, too—even the ones you'd normally ignore.

Your body can also distract you. Something itches, or that bruise on your elbow mysteriously starts hurting again.

The biggest distractions of all are the ones that start **inside your own head.** Between one breath and the next, you might find yourself thinking about something that happened yesterday, or worrying about something that hasn't happened—but *might*.

Staying focused—even for five breaths—can feel like trying to balance a coin on its edge. It just won't stay where you put it. That's perfectly normal! Wandering is what brains naturally do.

In fact, there's no reason to feel bad about losing your focus. Why? Because in this exercise, staying as focused as a laser beam isn't the goal anyway. The goal is trying to notice each time your mind wanders. When that happens, you can bring your attention back to your breathing—gently—exactly the way you'd bring your puppy back.

Calling back your focus this way is exercise for your brain. So each time you notice that you've lost track, it's actually a reason to smile to yourself. You've just made your "attention muscle" a little bit stronger!

41

Getting Stronger

Try these other ways to flex your attention muscles.

Drawing on Your Imagination

Sketching or coloring can be a great way to find focus and feel calmer. Doing it without paper or pencils works just as well! Close your eyes and imagine drawing something in the air in front of you: pretty patterns, fantasy creatures, your own beloved pet. Imagine yourself drawing each line, one at a time, and see if you can keep what you've already "drawn" in your head as you add more. Whenever you lose track, just pick up your mental pencil and start again.

The Sounds Around You

Sit quietly for, say, three minutes and try to notice every single sound around you—whether it's loud or barely there. Can you hear a dog barking or water running? Is anyone talking or making other sounds, like coughing or yawning? When you notice a sound, listen carefully and describe it in your head. Is it high or low? Is it snappy or scratchy? Try to stay tuned until the sound fades or until you notice a different sound.

Walk This Way

When you're feeling too bouncy to sit and focus on sounds or your breath, try this. All you need are your own two feet! Choose a spot where you can walk at least ten steps without bumping into anything. Then start putting one foot in front of the other. Walk slowly or quickly—it's up to you. Notice how each step feels. Can you feel your leg as it lifts your foot? Can you feel the ground as you step down? Walk back and forth five or ten times. Each time you catch your attention wandering, steer it back to the next step.

Five Senses, One Bite

The next time you take a bite of your favorite fruit, imagine that you must tell a friend who has never even seen this fruit what it's like. What color is it? Is it heavy or light in your hand? How does it smell? Is it smooth or bumpy? When you bite, does it crunch or make a slurping sound? How does it feel in your mouth? Is it crisp or soft? Take your time chewing. Does it taste tart or sweet, or a little of both? When you use all your senses to focus—*really* focus—on a familiar food, you might find that it tastes new to you, too.

Almost anything can feel fresher and more interesting if you truly pay attention to it. In fact, experts say that almost nothing feels better than the feeling of being completely tuned in to what you are seeing, hearing, or doing.

The Big Lie:

Icandoalotofstuffallatonce

Does this sound familiar? You're planning your history presentation on your mom's laptop while music videos run in another window on the screen. Texts blip onto your phone every few minutes, so of course you read them. You're thinking, "I can get my homework done and have fun and weigh in on everyone's photos all at the same time. No problem!"

And when a parent or teacher says it's not good to do so many things at once, you might also be thinking something like this: "Well, Ms. Shakerag didn't even have a laptop or a smartphone growing up, so she just hasn't had as much practice. It's different for me."

Think again. Scientists have measured what happens in people's brains when they're multitasking. They've discovered that your brain can focus on only one thing at a time, which means it has to quickly switch back and forth between jobs, over and over again. Each time your brain makes this shift, it takes extra effort. The switching leaves a kind of mental gap that allows important things to get overlooked.

The result? You have a harder time remembering things, and you make more mistakes. (Uh-oh. You just texted that you've got a "beak" on your face, when you meant to say "breakout.")

Probably not.

It turns out that people who make a habit of dividing their attention between phones and computers and tablets may *feel* more comfortable keeping lots of plates spinning, but they actually get worse at focusing on one thing. They have a harder time tuning out things they don't want to pay attention to—like dripping faucets or little brothers.

Here's the craziest thing: The people who *thought* they were the best at multitasking were actually the ones who made the most mistakes! Multitasking is a trickster. It makes you blind to how you're really doing.

45

A Multitasking Trick

It goes without saying that you shouldn't multitask when you're babysitting, riding a bike, or doing anything where safety—your own or someone else's—is at stake. But when you just need to concentrate on homework, try the **15-5 Plan.** Here's how it works . . .

Turn off any screen or close any window you don't absolutely need. Set a timer for 15 minutes and zero in on your work. Give your whole heart and brain to it. This will be easier because you know you are only going to work in short bursts.

When the timer rings, give yourself a break for exactly 5 minutes: Grab a drink, stretch, do jumping jacks, or check your phone.

When the 5 minutes are up, go straight back to your project. (No dillydallying!) Keep alternating that way—15 on, 5 off—for an hour or so, or until you're finished for the day. All those texts and posts will still be there on your phone, right where you left them.

A Place for Daydreams

Do you have to be tuned in all the time? No way!

Any girl who's ever multiplied fractions, practiced the oboe, or worked to pitch strikes in softball knows that brains quickly get tired from focusing. Like any other part of you, your brain needs rest.

What you may not know is that even switching to things that feel fun or interesting—such as playing video games, reading a book in your fave series, or clicking your way through a social media thread—really can't give a girl's brain the vacation it needs. That's because focusing on these kinds of things still draws on many of the same parts of your brain as focusing on work.

Instead, experts say the best mental rest happens when you're doing something that allows your mind to wander wherever it wants. Spending time in nature is a great way to give your mind some space for daydreams. So is doing a simple craft, like knitting or beading, or drawing patterns. And—surprise!—so is doing simple chores, like sweeping or raking leaves, as long as you don't have to think much.

Experts say your brain solves some problems best in daydream mode—when you don't feel as if you're thinking hard about anything! Many famous scientists have come up with some of their most important ideas while their minds were wandering. Sir Isaac Newton said he thought up the law of gravity while he was daydreaming under an apple tree.

What might *you* dream up in a daydream?

When I make someone else happy, I feel happy, too, and that's the best feeling in the world. —Leah

HAPPINESS HABIT 3

CARING AND CONNECTING

Born to Care

Have you ever made a silly face at a tiny baby only to have the baby lock eyes with you and make the same silly face right back? You can't help smiling.

Unlike some animals that can live on their own the moment they come into the world, human babies are born depending on others. A baby can't walk, talk, or feed herself. No human has ever survived without someone to care for her.

But babies have a special trick: Their brains are wired to reach out for kindness and caring by sharing emotions with others. Before they can do much else, babies can mimic a silly expression or smile back when someone smiles at them. It's one way a human being, no matter how small, can say, "Hey, we're alike. We're in this together. We're connected."

Babies get the care they need because human brains are wired to want to care and share. Of course, this is great for babies. But more than that, when we are caring and generous to anyone—whether a baby or a kid or a grown-up—we tend to feel great ourselves, too. That's why one of the surest ways to be happy is to have a habit of caring, a habit of kindness.

What *Is* Kindness?

Well, it's not just about being polite or "nice." And you don't need to have an outgoing personality or to smile nonstop. Kindness is much simpler, and a whole lot more powerful.

Kindness is about really, truly wanting the best for someone else. It begins with understanding that, no matter how different someone might seem, she's still like you in all the most important ways: She gets sad, lonely, worried, or angry sometimes. She makes mistakes. And she wants to be happy, like you. When you feel these things deep down, you don't have to force yourself to be kind. You just can't help it.

You've probably already noticed one other important thing about kindness: It's only real if it's completely free.

If you're nice only so people won't be mad at you, or if you're understanding and generous only toward people you're friends with, it isn't exactly kindness at work. True kindness reaches past your group of friends. True kindness means doing something generous or caring without expecting anything in return—not even thanks.

Being kind lights her up on the inside, and that just feels good.

Still, a girl who tries to act with real kindness every chance she gets often *does* get something back.

Being kind can take her mind off her own worries, so she feels less stressed.

Being kind can help keep her body healthier, because it lowers blood pressure.

Being kind can help her feel connected to other people, so she feels less lonely.

Starting Off

Want to see where kindness can lead you? If so, the place to start is right where you are. Being kind to yourself first might sound backward. Maybe you think it's selfish to treat yourself kindly. Maybe you think kindness is something you can "use up," so you shouldn't use too much for yourself.

Not true! In fact, it's pretty hard to treat anyone else with kindness if you aren't gentle with yourself first. This is easier to understand if you think of kindness like a clean, cool, stream of water on a hot day. It just keeps flowing, so there's always more. But if you haven't filled your own water bottle, how can you share it with anyone who's thirsty?

Do You Treat Yourself with Kindness?

Think of a time when you messed up or didn't succeed at something. How did you talk to yourself when that happened? Choose up to six words from the top of the next page that fit your inner voice best.

encouraging mean
sympathetic impatient
interested intolerant
irritable uncaring firm judging
soothing angry accepting respectful
forgiving understanding insulting caring
annoyed harsh thoughtful blaming
reflective critical tender
reassuring gentle
demanding
supportive

What color were the words you chose?

Mostly blue: Like everyone, you feel bad when things go wrong, but talking to yourself with kindness helps you get back on track. You know that absolutely everyone flubs up sometimes, which keeps you from feeling alone or singled out when it happens to you.

A mix of blue and green: You know it's important to be gentle with yourself, but sometimes you forget. A girl whose inner voice tends to be critical or uncaring may be harder on herself than necessary. Unkind words to yourself make it harder to recover when something sets you back.

Mostly green: When things are tough, you may struggle to treat yourself with kindness. You may feel like you're the only one who's hurting or who messes up—and that makes you feel even worse. It can help to remember that sooner or later everyone struggles with something. And while it's normal to feel embarrassed, angry, or sad, you don't have to put yourself down in order to learn from your mistakes. Instead, try telling yourself something like this: "It's normal to hit a rough patch now and then. If I'm gentle with myself, it will help me move on."

Growing Kinder

I *want* to be kinder. But what if I just don't *feel* that way?

Right now, you might be asking yourself this question. If so, you are not alone. Almost everyone feels like this from time to time.

It probably won't surprise you to learn that kindness and understanding—toward yourself *and* others—will grow if you practice them. They are "mind muscles" you can strengthen. The activities on this page are good ways to get started. As you feel your kindness muscle getting stronger, you may find yourself acting in kind ways without even thinking about it!

She's Like Me

Are you butting heads with a friend? Do you sometimes struggle to get along with your sister, a classmate, or a kid on the bus? This easy exercise has helped many people feel better and do better with difficult relationships.

First, picture what the other person looks like. Then try to keep that picture in your head while you think about the ways you and she are very much alike . . .

Just like me, Braeden has a body.

Just like me, Braeden feels lonely, scared, mad, or embarrassed sometimes.

Just like me, Braeden wants to be happy.

Just like me, Braeden has feelings.

Just like me, Braeden wants people to like her.

This exercise is a way of reminding yourself that you and another person are part of the same big club—the Human Beings Club. It can help you feel more connected to anyone in your life.

Make a Wish

You can do this with a real fountain—but it works with an imaginary one, too.

Start by thinking of someone you really, really love. Maybe it's a parent or a best friend. Or maybe it's Snippet, your cuddly little cockapoo. Picture the person or pet in your mind, and let yourself feel all the warm and smiley feelings. Think about how much you love and wish good things for him or her.

Now see if you can take that warm, smiley wish and send it back to yourself. Imagine you are tossing a penny in a fountain and making this wish:

"I hope I have a lot of happy things in my life."

Next, imagine tossing a penny and making a wish for someone you know and like:

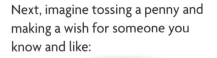

"I hope Farida stays safe on her trip and has a great time."

Your next penny can be for someone you might not know well:

"I hope Mr. Stitzel, the bus driver, has a good day and that kids don't hassle him too much."

You can keep tossing imaginary pennies and sending kind wishes to anyone you can think of, even people you don't know at all. You can even send a wish to the birds in the park—

"I hope you find lots to sing about today."

—or that new tree on your street—

"I hope you grow straight and strong."

You will never run out of pennies—or wishes.

59

Kindness Is . . .

Saying sorry when you're wrong.

Cutting your brownie in half and sharing it.

Messaging a compliment to someone you don't usually compliment . . .

and not arguing when someone compliments *you.*

Cheering someone on in gym class.

Helping someone else learn something you're good at: setting up video games, multiplying fractions, drawing noses.

Not saying the judgey, critical thing you can't help thinking.

Carrying in the groceries without being asked.

Asking, "How do you feel?"

Hiding a coin or polished stone somewhere outside, knowing someone will find it.

Learning the names of the crossing guard and lunch helpers. Using their names when you say hello.

Doing a chore when it's not your turn.

Asking, "How can I help?"

Letting your brother or sister go first.

Feeding the neighbors' fish when they're away.

Giving someone the benefit of the doubt.

Sticking up for someone who's being teased.

Walking your dog an extra block.

Making a get-well card for someone who's sick.

Calling your grandmother or grandfather just to say hi.

Bringing a bag along on a hike and gathering up the trash you spot.

Deciding not to complain about anything—not one single thing!—for a day.

Putting down your phone and chatting with the people you're *with*.

Thinking of one nice thing about a classmate you don't especially like.

Learning what's great about a holiday your family *doesn't* celebrate.

Donating your outgrown books for the library book sale.

Sticking a friendly note on someone's locker.

Leaving the last piece for someone else.

Buying lemonade from a little kid's stand.

Passing along nice words that someone else said . . .

Encouraging the kid who messed up . . .

even when that kid is *you*.

but stopping gossip in its tracks.

61

It's Contagious!

Believe it or not, you can catch kindness from someone else, just like you can catch the sniffles. Experts say that when someone is being kind, others tend to follow her lead, one after another—often without even knowing why! A single act of kindness can start a chain reaction that ripples through your family, your school, or even the world around you.

1:17 p.m. Amir notices that Lucy forgot her graph paper.

Here, use some of mine.

I owe you one.

Are you ready for the test?

1:38 p.m. Lucy is friendly to Cerisse, a shy girl she doesn't usually talk to.

EarthSavers

3:36 p.m. The EarthSavers love Cerisse's idea for a Manatee Splash car wash to raise money for endangered species.

We can charge extra to vacuum inside the cars...

Cool!

Yeah!

3:10 p.m. Cerisse feels brave enough to sign up for the EarthSavers after-school club.

3 weeks later. The car wash raises lots of donations, and the kids have a bubbly blast.

Awesome!

CAR WASH VACUUM

Why not start your own game of "kindness tag?" Even if it doesn't change the world, it will always change at least one person—you.

63

to Help

...nd you've done for someone else ...nything in return? How did it feel?

I think... are you?

I try to compliment at least one person every day because it makes me feel good inside.
—Hannah

When my grandmother's cat died, she got a new puppy. She didn't have the money to pay for the little dog's vet bills, so I gave her some of my money and also told her the money she spends on presents for me could instead be used to pay for the bills. My grandmother started crying because she was so happy, and it made me feel really warm inside to know I had just made someone very happy.
—Ayla

On a field trip, one girl only had $2, but drinks were $3. She was dying of thirst, so I gave her a dollar to buy a drink. My friends asked me why I gave it to her, and I said it was the right thing to do.
—Emily

I watched my younger brother while my parents were at a concert. It was fun, even though he can be mean, and though I knew my mom was not going to take me out for ice cream or anything special.
—Jordan

I helped a classmate I don't know very well with a science project when she needed help. It made me feel good to help her, even if she's not my close friend.
—Belle

At the store there was this little old lady who couldn't get a cart and kept dropping her cane. While my mom got our groceries, I helped the lady get hers. She was so thankful that she bought us lunch! We have been friends ever since, so when she needs groceries my mom and I go and get ours with her.
—Sarah

When my friend got glasses, the boys called her mean names. So the next day I wore fake glasses, and they did the same thing to me. I asked them how they would like being called names if they got glasses. The next day they stopped. Now a lot of my friends have glasses, and no one teases them. I feel good knowing I stood up for my friend.
—Kate

My school was doing a coin drive to help end summer hunger. My best friend and I set up a lemonade stand by the pool to get more customers. After a weekend, we counted our money. We made $71.66! Now whenever I talk about it to my friends, I get a good feeling in my heart.
—Colleen

Most of the time there is never really a BIG thing I do out of kindness, just a lot of little things, like smiling, saying thank you, cleaning up dishes, etc. A big thing is only once, but little things you can do over and over again! And they make me feel proud.
—Misty

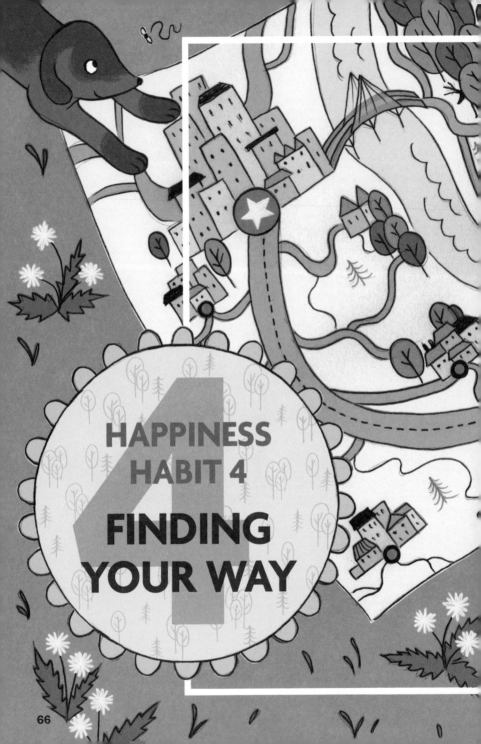

HAPPINESS HABIT 4
FINDING YOUR WAY

To reach her goals, a girl definitely needs confidence. I've seen that I can't just fix my weaknesses automatically. It takes time. But when I work at it, I discover more about myself. I'm learning that I have more strengths than I thought. —Kat

Stars to Steer By

Challenging myself

Finding beauty in the world

Growing spiritually

Saying how I think and feel

Being creative

Learning all I can

Trying new things

How do you get to a place you've never been? These days, many people use an app on their phones, a friendly voice that tells them exactly which turns to take. But long ago, before people had smartphones and even before parts of the world were mapped, sailors used the stars. By looking to the sky and tracking the stars' positions, sailors figured out where they were—and how to get where they wanted to go.

As you get older, you're trying to find your way to places you've never been. And since no app in the world can tell you exactly how to do that, you need a few stars to guide you, too. When you feel lost or out of place, the stars that keep you steady are your values, the things that matter to you most.

Being active

Being a true friend

Staying healthy and strong

Being honest

Loving my family

Making new friends

Improving my skills

Being generous

Caring for the planet

Being kind

What are the stars you steer by? You might find some of your own values on this page. Or you might dream up some that are completely your own. All that matters is that they come straight from your heart.

Write down your own guiding stars and keep them where you can see them: on a mirror, in a pretty notebook, or over your desk. Keep updating your list as you grow and change.

Seeing Your Strengths

Q: What else can help a girl stay steady as she grows?

A: Knowing the best parts of herself—and being able to call on them in good times and bad.

You're still building your skills and discovering your talents. The things you're good at today are a small fraction of the things you'll be good at down the road. But every girl has a few ways in which she seems to shine practically from the start, a handful of things that seem knit right in to her personality. Experts who have studied these built-in "character strengths" say that the more you use yours, the easier it is to feel happy.

How can you learn more about your own best self?

One way is to ask someone who knows you—such as a teacher, a parent, or another adult you trust—to help you identify your strongest qualities.

Another way is to ask yourself the same question the next time you are feeling very confident or proud of something you did. What abilities were you using in that moment? (Hint: You might have been using more than one.)

Finding Your Fit

You're getting to know your strengths. Now, you wonder, how and where do you use them? Figuring that out can be tricky. You can't just follow your friends: The best fit for your unique combination of strengths may not be the same as theirs. It may not be what your parents or teachers want for you either. Chances are, you may not even know what's the best fit for you and what's not.

There's only one way to find out. You have to try things on, the same way you'd try on a pair of shoes. You have to do things—sometimes lots of things—before you know what really fits. Go out for cross-country. Try your hand at calligraphy. Sign up for the school poetry slam. Don't rule anything out just because it's unfamiliar or because you aren't good at it yet.

Whatever you're trying, remember that what matters is *not* how things wind up in the end. Did you win or lose? Did other people like what you did? Those things aren't as important as you might think. It also doesn't matter if what you're doing seems easy or hard at first.

Instead, pay special attention to how you're feeling when you're doing things. From time to time, you'll feel frustrated, nervous, or tired. That's normal when you try something new. But look for other feelings, too: Do you feel curious? Challenged in a good way? More alive than when you're doing other things? Does time just fly by?

Above all, does it feel like there's a spark inside you that wants to grow bigger and brighter? That tiny spark is how you know it's a fit. It's your sign to keep going.

73

Stretching Yourself

Steer yourself in a happy direction by setting your sights on something you want to accomplish—and then reach toward it.

Your goal can be small.

"I want to learn how to paint awesome fingernail designs."

"I want to make friends with that shy girl who sits by herself at lunch."

Goals can also be **bigger** and take longer to prepare for or accomplish.

"I want to make a video about my favorite books."

"I want to ride a unicycle."

"I want to make the field hockey team."

Having a goal to work toward feeds happiness in lots of ways.

Goals can give a girl . . .

★ something to look forward to.

★ new friendships with other kids who have similar goals.

★ a way to get better at something that matters to her.

Most of all, having a goal that inspires you to stretch a little beyond what you can do now reminds you of one very important truth:

You never have to feel stuck. Ever.

In fact, the moment you begin taking steps toward a goal, you've begun to learn . . . and grow. And the girl who makes *any* progress—no matter how small—is always a different girl than the one who set the goal. She's that much wiser, stronger, and more confident. All it takes is a little persistence and patience.

Now or Later?

What are you willing to wait for?

1. Your friends say the Dragon Drop is the most awesome roller coaster ever. It looks like everyone at the park agrees: The line's a mile long! You're . . .

  a. moving on. The Dragon Drop's probably not that great anyway, and there's hardly anyone in line for the Toaster Coaster.

  b. staying put! Once you're up in the air, you'll have forgotten all about how long it took to get there.

2. There's a package behind the coats in the front closet, and the wrapping paper is kind of see-through. You think your birthday present might be inside it. When do you find out?

  a. Right this second, because you're going to peek!

  b. On your birthday. It won't be easy, but you'll stay away from that box.

3. You've sailed through your math homework, and now you're halfway through labeling the diagram of a cow's eye when—*ping!*—a text pops up on your phone. Your next move is to . . .

a. pick up the phone. Who wouldn't? You'll get back to the worksheet in a minute. (Or when your dad reminds you.)

b. figure out where "cornea" and "retina" go. You'll have more fun texting if you're homework-free.

4. There's nothing tastier than your uncle's special homemade four-cheese pineapple-pepperoni pizza. In fact, there's just one thing wrong with it:

a. The cheese always burns your mouth because you dig in too soon.

b. You have to let it cool down a bit before you can eat any!

5. You're with the school counselor, signing up for next year's electives. Ms. Dabble-Hernandez says if you take the math review class now, you'll find math much easier in high school. But it's up to you, she says. For fifth hour, you choose . . .

a. art class. You don't want things to be easier later; you want them more fun now.

b. math review. There are tons of cool art classes in high school, and you'll enjoy them more if you're confident with your other subjects.

6. After walking the neighbors' poodles for weeks, you finally have enough money for that fancy paint set—the "starter" set with 24 colors, anyway. Just four more dog walks and you'd have enough money for the 48-color set. Which one sounds best?

a. The 24-color set will do. You've waited long enough!

b. All 48 colors for you. What's a few more trips around the neighborhood with Thor and Spindrift when you're this close?!

DRAGON·DROP

Answers

Most of the questions don't have one right answer. If you're like most girls, you chose some a's and some b's. For some questions, it might have felt hard to choose what you'd do: go for what's closest or easiest (the **a** answers) or hang on for something better or more satisfying (the **b** answers). Maybe you'd choose differently on a different day, depending on your mood.

It might even feel like there are two girls inside your head—one who's okay with waiting, and one who wants it now. That's because, in a way, there are! One part of your brain is in charge of going for what looks, sounds, or feels good right this minute. Another part of the brain helps you wait, think of the future, and try again. Called the frontal cortex, this second part focuses on why it's worth waiting in order to get what really matters to you.

And guess what? You don't have to wait to help this part of your brain take charge. There are lots of ways you can help it along right this minute.

Power Up!

These little tricks help boost your willpower and put your goals within reach.

Take a Breather

Sometimes when you're doing something tough, your attention begins to wander and you don't even notice it's happened. So how can you steer back on track if you don't notice you've gone off it? Before starting a demanding task, try spending a minute or two doing one of the breathing or attention-strengthening exercises on pages 38–43. The more you practice these exercises, the better you'll get at noticing when you've lost sight of your goal.

Use Your Imagination

Imagine yourself in the future, when your hard work has paid off. Is your goal to finish eight beaded necklaces for the soccer club fund-raiser? Imagine yourself crimping the last bead in place. Picture how pretty the finished necklaces look on the display table.

Set the Stage

If you've got a tough task ahead, brainstorm ways to make it easier to stick with it. If texts tempt you, turn your phone off or leave it in another room. If you can't stop playing puppy videos when you're supposed to be memorizing the Preamble to the Constitution, ask your parents for help finding free web-blocking software. You can program it to keep you out of tempting sites for whatever amount of time you decide.

Have a Plan

Make a list of roadblocks you may hit on the way to your goal. (Be honest!) Then come up with a plan for getting around them. Use the words *if* and *then*: "If Priti comes over when I'm practicing, then I'll tell her I will call her in an hour." "If I start to get tired of reading the book, then I'll switch to working on the poster."

Don't Go It Alone

Let parents, teachers, and friends in on your goal. If other people know your heart's set on getting strong enough to climb Mt. Kettlebell, they'll probably love cheering you on as you train. And when your willpower starts to wane, you'll have a shoulder—or two or three—to lean on.

Yay!

Just Get Started

If you've ever struggled to get yourself to do something tough, it's a safe bet that someone, somewhere, has said words like this to you: Just get it done. But when the "it" is something big, like finishing a story you've been writing or getting in 40 laps at swim practice, getting it done may feel totally out of reach. Thinking this way might just make you want to pull the covers over your head.

What if you told yourself something different instead? What if all you had to do was get started? Ask yourself: What's the teeniest thing I can begin with? Can I swim one lap? Can I write one paragraph? One sentence? Can I practice trombone for two minutes? Once you've gone for two minutes, the next two—and the next two after that—will seem *much* easier.

In fantasy books, kids who accomplish amazing things usually call on magical help. When things get too tough, there's an enchanted ring or a wand or a string of special words that—*poof!*—make everything seem possible again.

What makes things possible in real life? You'll find all the magic you need in just two words: *keep going.* Do that, and before long you've done what you set out to do—one teeny, totally nonmagical step at a time.

Worth the Wait

What's something that took a lot of time or effort for you to accomplish? How did it feel?

I helped create a butterfly garden as a Girl Scout project. Planning it and caring for the plants was a lot of work. We would always help each other and laugh when it got tough. It was amazing when we finished it, and I loved watching the butterflies that came.

—Solenn

It took me half the summer last year to get all the swim strokes right so I would not get eliminated in competitions. This year, I practiced in the winter at an indoor pool. Hopefully, my swim team coaches will be proud of my hard work. I know I am!

—Kate

I set a goal to make it up a level in ballet, which I'd been trying to do for five years. This year, I finally reached my goal. When I blanked out onstage at the winter show, it was really a setback. But I'm still happy I reached my goal.

—Hailey

I wrote a long story in English. (My native language is Finnish.) Writing the story took a long time, and sometimes I felt like I'd never finish, especially when I couldn't write the fanciest words. I haven't shown the story to anyone yet, but I'm proud I did it.

—Ida

I'm teaching myself to do gymnastics. It's not as easy as in a regular gym because I don't have equipment except a few mats. Some skills took a LOT of hard work. Some I'm still learning. But I put my mind to it, and whenever I get a skill it takes me by surprise. I do it again to make sure I'm not dreaming!

—Chaya

I started an art and literature magazine for my school. It took a long time to get it moving. At first no one submitted any of their work. But after a few months people saw the potential and started submitting. Now it's really popular!

—Zlata

I broke my arm and couldn't bend it, so the doctor told me that I should exercise it. It hurt! It took a long time before I got used to the feeling. It still hurts here and there, but now I'm a lot better!

—Mary

It took me six days to canoe the entire Buffalo River with my dad and my sister. There were a lot of storms along the way, but we did it. I was so proud!

—Madison

I asked kids in my class to recycle the plastic water bottles they brought to school. Every day now, I come home with a backpack full of plastic water bottles to recycle. This is a big accomplishment.

—Cora

I take figure skating lessons, and my instructor taught me a new jump called the Lutz. I was super frustrated with it. But I kept practicing every minute I got, and I finally landed it! That taught me something: If something important is hard, just keep at it and improve yourself. One day, you WILL accomplish it!

—Maci

The little things that make you smile are way more important than they seem. If you rely on just one thing to make you happy, what happens when it's gone? If you focus on the little things, there'll always be something to bring you up when you are down.
—Zoe

HAPPINESS HABIT 5

LOOKING FOR WHAT'S GOOD

Hide and Seek

Any girl who's ever dug through a stack of papers in search of her social studies assignment or who's felt under her bed for her glasses already knows one important truth:

If you want to find something,

you've almost always got to look for it.

The good moments in your life are that way, too. They're practically everywhere. But they can be hard to see. If you don't make a point of seeking good things out—on purpose—they tend to sneak right by before you can enjoy them. They also don't stick as easily in your memory as bad things do.

Why can good things be so hard to notice and hang on to?

It's just the way brains work. Your brain is wired to protect you. To keep you safe, its fastest parts are devoted to looking out for problems—and not just big ones. Your brain is constantly looking for eensy-weensy problems, and even things that *seem* like they might be problems but really aren't.

These problem-finding parts of your brain work like a smoke detector, always sniffing the air for any sign of fire. As a result, your brain is super-good at tuning in to whatever's wrong.

But other parts of your brain can tune in to what's right, too.

Enjoying the Ride

No matter where you are or what you're doing, your brain is super busy. Information about the world around you floods in from your five senses, and your brain has to sort it all out, on the spot. Thoughts and opinions bubble up constantly about the things you see, hear, feel, taste, and smell.

It would be great if you could turn off all the mental noise the way you switch off a screechy hair dryer or an annoying song. But that's practically impossible. (Remember, it's just your brain doing its job.) Still, there is something you *can* do: You can choose which thoughts you'll focus on. You can decide to look for the little, positive thoughts that are bubbling up all the time, even though they don't normally attract as much attention. Often, this one simple choice can make all the difference between feeling grumpy and feeling great.

Will this girl have fun paddling? It all depends!

Gathering the Good

Now that you notice the good moments in your day, the next step is to really *enjoy* them. Here's how.

Pick Up the Pebble

Have you ever spotted a pretty pebble on the beach? Did you pick it up and really look at it, or did you just keep right on walking? This is a great way to think about the small, positive things that are happening all around you.

When someone is friendly to you, when you step into the shade on a hot day, when your baby sister makes you laugh, when you smell cinnamon rolls, or when you just have a nice thought, take a moment to hold on to the tiny, warm feeling it gives you. Can you feel a smile spread over your face, or a little extra bounce in your step? Really let that feeling sink in to your heart. Then imagine tucking that small, good moment in your pocket, just like a little treasure to carry with you.

Count to Three

At night while you're putting on your pajamas, press a mental "replay" button on your day and look for three positive things that happened. Don't be choosy! Anything that felt nice, made you smile, or merely caught your interest is worth including:

1. Anders said hi to me. Twice!

2. Mr. Woolwrap liked my debate topic.

3. Who knew how much fun square dancing would be?

It's also fine to include things that you might not describe as sunny or funny, but that are positive in a less-obvious way. For example, if you're going through a rough patch with a friend, struggling in school, or just not feeling well, your mental list might look more like this:

1. I know Quinn and I will get through it.

2. Ms. Blotz can see that I'm trying.

3. The nap I took seemed to help.

Once you've thought of three things, challenge yourself to a memory game:

Can you remember each one in the morning?

Salute the Small Stuff

There's no reason to save celebrations for holidays and other once-in-a-while events. Inviting your friends and family to share in the tiny things that bring you happiness is a surefire way to help good feelings grow. So why not invite everyone to join in a round of applause or high fives when . . .

Your hamster, Gertrude, makes it all the way through the cereal box maze you made.

You finish the 10-foot scarf you were crocheting.

You didn't bite your nails all day.

You see the first red leaves of autumn or the first tulips in spring.

You found your lucky scrunchie.

It's your goldfish's birthday.

You discover a dollar in one of your pockets.

You got your braces off.

You balanced on your unicycle for 16 whole seconds.

You get cool Ms. Clinkenberry for math.

You got your braces *on*. (You'll have healthy teeth, and isn't that worth celebrating?)

Celebrate Each Day

Who knows? There may already be a special day for some of the little things that make you smile, and someone, somewhere, may love celebrating it, too. Check out these silly holidays and add one—or more—to your calendar.

JANUARY

8   Bubble Bath Day
16   Appreciate a Dragon Day
20   Penguin Awareness Day

FEBRUARY

7   Play Your Ukulele Day
15   National Gumdrop Day
26   Tell a Fairy Tale Day

MARCH

2   Old Stuff Day
10   Middle Name Pride Day
23   Puppy Day

APRIL

8   Draw a Picture of a Bird Day
14   Look Up in the Sky Day
23   World Party Day

MAY

12 Limerick Day
13 Frog Jumping Day
16 Love a Tree Day

JUNE

6 National Yo-Yo Day
11 Corn on the Cob Day
27 Sunglasses Day

JULY

10 Teddy Bear Picnic Day
18 World Juggling Day
29 National Lasagna Day

AUGUST

3 Watermelon Day
7 Sisters' Day
30 Frankenstein Day

SEPTEMBER

19 International Talk Like a Pirate Day
25 National Comic Book Day

OCTOBER

1 Balloons Around the World Day
17 Wear Something Gaudy Day

NOVEMBER

8 Tongue Twister Day
11 Origami Day
16 Button Day

DECEMBER

8 Pretend to be a Time Traveler Day
16 Chocolate-Covered Anything Day

Don't see what you love? Make up your own holiday!

Feeling Down?

Of course, some days you don't feel like celebrating, and there's nothing wrong with that. Tuning in to what's good doesn't mean pushing away painful or unhappy feelings when you have them. It doesn't mean trying to convince yourself that you aren't feeling crummy when you are.

That's because tough emotions—sadness, worry, embarrassment, guilt, anger, envy, boredom, and fear—have really important jobs. They are your brain's way of nudging you to . . .

look carefully at some part of your life.

stay safe.

get something done.

remember something that needs to be remembered.

There are lots of games you can't play if cards are missing from the deck. And you need all of your emotions—even the yucky ones—to be able to "deal" with life. You need them all to respond well to everything that happens to you.

Knowing this doesn't make difficult feelings disappear. But understanding that feelings have a purpose can help you handle them. The breathing and body exercises on pages 22–27 of this book are great places to start. Once your stormy feelings have settled a bit, you'll be ready to begin listening—as closely and carefully as you can—to the messages they might be trying to send.

Reading Your Feelings

Every feeling speaks its own language.

Emotions communicate with you by sending specific signals to your body. But what if they sent letters instead? What would they say? Match these letters to the feelings that might have sent them.

Worry *Sadness* Embarrassment
Envy Anger Guilt *Boredom*

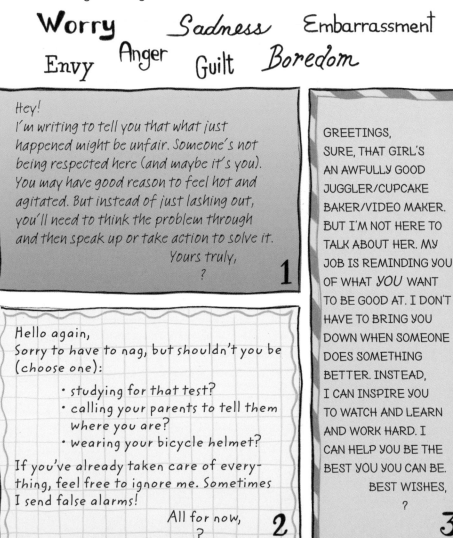

1

Hey!
I'm writing to tell you that what just happened might be unfair. Someone's not being respected here (and maybe it's you). You may have good reason to feel hot and agitated. But instead of just lashing out, you'll need to think the problem through and then speak up or take action to solve it.

Yours truly,
?

2

Hello again,
Sorry to have to nag, but shouldn't you be (choose one):

- studying for that test?
- calling your parents to tell them where you are?
- wearing your bicycle helmet?

If you've already taken care of everything, feel free to ignore me. Sometimes I send false alarms!

All for now,
?

3

GREETINGS,
SURE, THAT GIRL'S AN AWFULLY GOOD JUGGLER/CUPCAKE BAKER/VIDEO MAKER. BUT I'M NOT HERE TO TALK ABOUT HER. MY JOB IS REMINDING YOU OF WHAT *YOU* WANT TO BE GOOD AT. I DON'T HAVE TO BRING YOU DOWN WHEN SOMEONE DOES SOMETHING BETTER. INSTEAD, I CAN INSPIRE YOU TO WATCH AND LEARN AND WORK HARD. I CAN HELP YOU BE THE BEST YOU YOU CAN BE.

BEST WISHES,
?

Hi there,

Whoops! The mistake you just made was a doozy. We know you didn't mean it. The red-faced, hide-in-a-corner feeling you have now is our way of helping you (a) apologize quickly, (b) try to solve the problem, and (c) remember not to make the same mistake again. Now we've got to run. Absolutely everyone makes mistakes, so we're terribly, terribly busy!

Respectfully,
? and ?

4

To whom it may concern,
Ho-hum. I know why you're itching to look at your phone or look in the refrigerator instead of reading the rest of this note. You want me to go away! But you shouldn't brush me off so fast. I'm your signal to reach out for a real challenge, not easy entertainment. I rarely bug a girl who's solving a problem, striving for a goal, or doing something creative.

Cheers,
?

5

Dear friend,
When you hear from me, it's for the worst reason ever. You've lost something, or someone. But painful as I can be, I can also bring out the best in you. I force you to think deeply, to reach out to others for comfort, and to treasure all the good things you've still got. And by breaking hearts, I open them. A girl who's faced the ache I bring is a girl who's stronger and wiser and more understanding than she could be any other way.

Love always,
?

6

Answers: 1. Anger, 2. Worry, 3. Envy, 4. Embarrassment and Guilt, 5. Boredom, 6. Sadness

How did you do? If you didn't get them all, don't worry. The positive messages in negative feelings can be really tricky to see, but it's well worth trying. Tough emotions don't like to be ignored. The more closely you can listen to what they are trying to tell you, the more quickly they will probably move on.

Grateful Is Great

Tough feelings are easier to ride out if you have a full storehouse of positive feelings to call on when you need them. You can start filling your storehouse right this second with one simple word:

Thanks.

You probably learned to say thank you when you were little. When you got a bit older, your parents might have insisted you write thank-you notes for gifts you received—even for those crumbly bars of soap that Great Aunt Dode gave you. You said thank you because it was the right thing. You still do, because it still is.

Great Aunt Dode
1029 Obideau Way
Drewbyville, Virginia

Wow!

But *feeling* thankful, down to the tips of your toes, is something completely different. Feeling thankful is noticing that lots of things in your life—almost everything, in fact—are like gifts, too, since they come from somewhere else or someone other than you. Feeling thankful is not taking the good stuff for granted. It's letting yourself be amazed by anything that's kind or generous or beautiful. Feeling thankful is like carrying a little "wow" around in your heart.

Like kindness, feeling thankful just plain feels great. But experts have found that people who make it a habit to be grateful get other rewards, too. They have more energy, and they reach their goals more often. They feel less lonely. They even sleep better!

Not feeling thankful? By now you've probably guessed that, like attention and kindness, gratitude is a muscle you can strengthen. It's like a flower you can grow.

Thanks a Lot!

Here are some ways to help gratitude bloom.

The Eyes Have It

When you say thanks to someone, even for something tiny, look the person in the eye. You might be surprised by how different it feels.

Keep It Going

Think of ways to pay back someone's kindness when they least expect it. Better yet, think about ways you can "pay it forward." By returning the favor to a *different* person, you keep the gratitude going.

Track It Back

Next time you do something you love—sip an apple-berry smoothie, hear a great song on the car radio, snuggle up in your favorite jammies—try to think of everyone who played a part in bringing that one thing into your life.

For example, when you slip a new T-shirt over your head, you might start by thinking about . . .

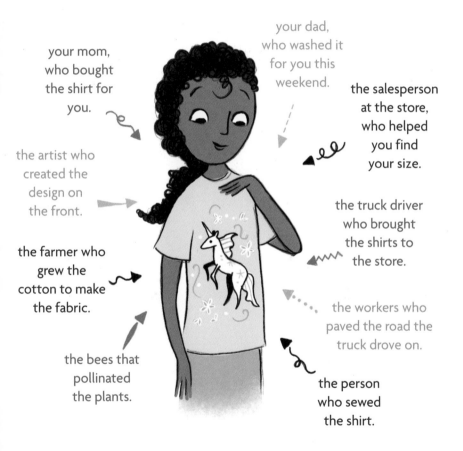

your mom, who bought the shirt for you.

your dad, who washed it for you this weekend.

the salesperson at the store, who helped you find your size.

the artist who created the design on the front.

the truck driver who brought the shirts to the store.

the farmer who grew the cotton to make the fabric.

the workers who paved the road the truck drove on.

the bees that pollinated the plants.

the person who sewed the shirt.

You get the idea. Make a game of it. See how many people (or other living things) you can come up with. When you think of everyone who had a hand in making one nice thing possible for you, it's pretty hard to feel lonely—and it's almost impossible not to feel thankful.

Grateful YOU

Are there small things that add to your life in big ways?
Are there big things that make your heart sing?

I'm grateful for my books and the library.
—Kerilynn

I came from another country. My friends and I often disagree on stuff, but without them, I'd feel pretty lonely. I'm extremely grateful for them.
—Sofia

My brother has autism and can't talk. He doesn't live with my family, so I feel very thankful when he can come home for visits on the weekends. I love his smile, and it always makes my day.
—Kelly

I have life-threatening food allergies and asthma. Here's the good news: I have started training service dogs to be medical alert and response dogs. They are helping me become independent. My health issues and my service dogs are part of who I am, so I'm grateful for them both.
—Moira

I love my siblings! They don't always agree with me or listen to me, but I still try to love them and be thankful for them.
—Maggie

The thing that makes me grateful is that my sweet and wild brother was adopted by our family. I love him.
—Carson

We just got a puppy after three years of my wanting one. So I KNOW I have to be thankful for that!
—Ellie

I always feel grateful for the things that people do for me, but sometimes it's hard for me to remember to say thank you. I want to get better at it.
—Jemma

I have been singing with the same choir for seven years. I am grateful because now singing is a big part of my life.
—Rachel

I find it hard to feel thankful sometimes because it feels like things always go the wrong way. I know that's not true, but when I'm at a low point it's hard to appreciate what I have.
—Korra

I'm grateful that we live in a place where we have clean water, and medicine, and freedom to choose what we want to. A lot of countries don't have that.
—Riley

I treasure the little things in life, like the sunny day, the opened door, the delicious breakfast, and the laugh with my BFF.
—AllieBeth

If you're trying to start a good habit, it helps to think about how glad you'll be if you do it. Also, make it fun!
—Helen

HAPPINESS HABIT 6

KEEPING A GOOD THING GOING

Making It Stick

Now that you've almost finished reading this book, you know a lot of great ways to care for your mind, to help keep it both healthy and happy. But here's something you probably already knew before you started: Reading about anything is only a beginning.

You could read dozens of books about snowboarding, for example, and still not really know how to swoosh down a hill. To know something—truly know it—you have to actually *experience* it. You have to discover it for yourself.

Maybe you've already started following some of the tips you've read about in this book. But maybe, like lots and lots of girls, you sometimes find it hard to remember to do them— even when you know how fantastic they'll feel.

This is where it helps to have a few reminders. Little tricks like these help make habits stick.

Create an Inspiration Station

Clear a small spot in your room, and make an arrangement of items that remind you of what's important or joyful or beautiful in your life. It might be the feather you found on a walk, a quote from a book or person that inspires you, or a funny photo of your pet. Not enough room in your room? Make a scrapbook or poster using drawings, photos, or pictures clipped from magazines instead.

Make a Game of It

Choose something that happens several times during your day, and use it as a reminder for any habit you want to build. You could decide to focus on one full breath each time you switch on a light. You could decide to remember one thing you're grateful for each time you walk through a classroom door or see your favorite model of car on the road.

Watch the Goodness Grow

Keep a glass jar on your dresser. Each time you do something kind or follow another happiness habit, add a marble, button, brightly colored slip of paper, or snip of yarn to the jar. Before long, you'll have a colorful reminder of just how much good there is in your life.

Create a Code Word

Choose a secret word or phrase to remind yourself to notice what's good about the moment you're in. Then, when you're struggling to keep your perspective, just whisper those words to yourself: *Find the treasure. One good thing. Look around you.*

Before too long, you may discover that you don't need reminders to take time to relax, to tune in to what you're doing, to act with kindness, or to be open to what's good around you, because it's become automatic. Congratulations! Happiness has become your habit. You can dance the steps without thinking . . .

Do you have stories to share about your own happiness habits?
Send them to:
Editor, *Your Happiest YOU*
American Girl
8400 Fairway Place
Middleton, WI 53562

All comments and suggestions received by American Girl may be used without compensation or acknowledgment. We're sorry, but photos can't be returned.

Here are some other American Girl books you might like.

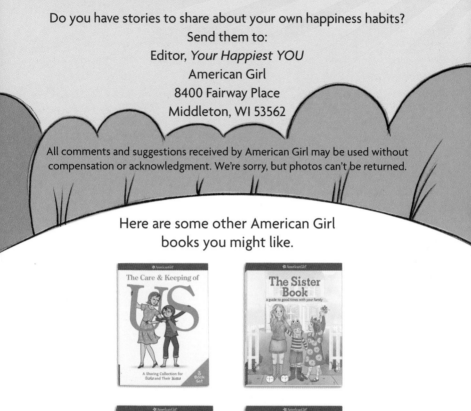

Each sold separately. Find more books online at americangirl.com.

Parents, request a FREE catalogue at **americangirl.com/catalogue.**
Sign up at **americangirl.com/email** to receive the latest news and exclusive offers.

Discover online games, quizzes, activities,
and more at **americangirl.com/play**

Resources

The experts whose ideas are mentioned in this book are people who study what's known as *positive psychology*, or the science of mental well-being. Books by and about these experts are listed below, along with online resources offering more information about other ideas in each section.

Growing Up Happy

centerhealthyminds.org

greatergood.berkeley.edu

Happiness: Unlocking the Mysteries of Psychological Wealth, by Ed Diener and Robert Biswas-Diener

The How of Happiness, by Sonja Lyubomirsky

Letting It Settle

Full Catastrophe Living, by Jon Kabat-Zinn

Tuning In

Child's Mind, by Christopher Willard

The Mindful Child, by Susan Kaiser Greenland

Rapt: Attention and the Focused Life, by Winifred Gallagher

Caring and Connecting

Lovingkindness: The Revolutionary Art of Happiness, by Sharon Salzberg

Self-Compassion, by Kristin Neff

Finding Your Way

Flourish, by Martin E.P. Seligman

Flow: The Psychology of Optimal Experience, by Mihaly Csikszentmihalyi

viacharacter.org

The Willpower Instinct, by Kelly McGonigal

Looking for What's Good

Positivity, by Barbara L. Fredrickson

Keeping a Good Thing Going

Making Habits, Breaking Habits, by Jeremy Dean

The Power of Habit, by Charles Duhigg

About the Author

Judy Woodburn is an avid student of the science of mental well-being and has practiced mindfulness meditation for more than 25 years. She is a co-author of *A Smart Girl's Guide: Worry: How to Feel Less Stressed and Have More Fun*, published by American Girl.

About the Consultants

Jane Annunziata, PsyD, is a clinical psychologist specializing in children. She is the author of many mental health and wellness books for children.

Lori Gustafson, MS, develops and implements mindfulness-based training in educational settings. She focuses on practices that cultivate kindness and attention, and that support the well-being of children.